Student Plays presents . . . two short college plays.

Stravinsky's Kitchen

and

Honoring the Hijacker

☞

☞

☞   ☞

<u>Copyright information. Please read!</u>

☞ About Student Plays ☜

Student Plays consists of **John Glass, Jackie Jernigan,** and **Dominic Torres.** We are a group of playwrights and directors that have written scripts for elementary school through college. We are proud of the variety of ages that our scripts serve.

Student Plays has "creepy" plays, and we also have Latino-themed plays. These are scripts that focus on Latino youths and the Latino experience. Any school can perform a Latino-themed play: it just requires a general introduction and basic exposure to the Spanish language, something that most schools and students already have.

To contact *Student Plays* or to communicate with one of the playwrights, simply email us at john@studentplays.org.

STRAVINSKY'S KITCHEN

\- -

A short dramedy for high school or college

by
John Glass

www.studentplays.org
john@studentplays.org

Stravinsky's Kitchen

☆ Characters ☆

BO   Twenties or thirties. Jerk.

LUKE   Twenties or thirties. Passive. Kind
                   and jovial.

STRAVINSKY   The Russian composer himself. In
                   his seventies/eighties.

The setting is the kitchen of a house in Los Angeles, the home of famous composer Igor Stravinsky. The time is the early 1970s. There is a table/island with a cutting board, crackers, garlic, potatoes, and other simple food items. On another table sits a cupful of pencils, magazines, a radio/ boombox, and other typical kitchen clutter.

On the far end of one side of the stage is a small dividing wall, and on the other side of this is a closet-style pantry. In the play, BO and LUKE peek out at the kitchen from this pantry. The wall can be a simple arrangement of chairs and a table, or even a construction of paper/cardboard, something that could easily be taken on and off the stage. There is a chef's hat and a tiny container of either olive oil, pepper, or salt inside the pantry.

Acknowledgements

Stravinsky's Kitchen was first performed on August 7, 2013 at Stage Door Theatre in Anaheim, California. The play was part of Orange County's New Voices Summer Festival. Playwright John Glass thanks the playwrights and directors of New Voices for helping bring *Stravinsky's Kitchen* to life.

The play is dedicated to the leadership and humor of playwright John Lane, who once actually did enter the kitchen of composer Igor Stravinsky.

At RISE: As the lights go up, BO and LUKE have just entered the house and are rummaging through the objects on the small table.

LUKE: Look at all this stuff!

BO: Stop screwing around. Help me look for it!

LUKE: Relax. It's not every day I get to enter a celebrity's house.

BO: Celebrity, my ass. More like pretentious Russian tightwad. Come on, keep looking. It's in a white envelope.

LUKE: *(Picks up pencil, plays with it.)* Does Mr. Stravinsky conduct with these?

BO: Luke! Stop! *(Knocks cup of pencils over.)* You imbecile! See what you made me do?

LUKE: We'll just pick them up. No big deal.

BO: I should have done this alone. This is all one huge mistake.

LUKE: Bo, you were scared to come in here by yourself!

BO: Oh, shut up and help me clean this up. *(Beat.)* Luke! What's that noise?

LUKE: Is he here?

BO: Shit! I don't know! *(He strains to hear if there's more noise.)* Okay, this is *not* happening!

LUKE: What do we do?

BO: Come on! Follow me!

LUKE: Ohhh! We're going to go to jail!!

BO: Shut up and come on!

> *(They scramble inside the pantry. Enter STRAVINSKY. He puts down his keys and newspaper, and begins to prepare a meal. He is gradually aggravated at how certain items are not in the proper place.)*

BO: I can't BELIEVE this! Stravinsky's supposed to be out of town. *(He watches him through the peephole.)*

LUKE: What are you doing? Can you see him?

BO: Shhhhh!! *(Pause.)* I cut a little hole in the sheetrock so I could come in here and smoke.

LUKE: You did what?

BO: I cut this little hole so that I could come in here and smoke. You know. So I can take a break whenever I want. I watch in case he comes into the kitchen.

LUKE: *(Looking.)* This is groovy!

BO: Quiet! He might hear us! You have to whisper! *(Pause)* What the hell's he doing here? He's supposed to be in Portland.

LUKE: I think he's going to cook something.

STRAVINSKY: American jackass. Doesn't leave anything where it should be.

LUKE: Does he know how to cook?

BO: I don't know. I always do it for him.

LUKE: How long do you think he'll be here?

(BO turns around, paces in anger.)

BO: I don't know. This sucks! We could be in here for hours!

LUKE: Hours?

BO: Well, *yeah*! You see what he's doing, don't you? He's not just making a sandwich.

LUKE: Well, he might be. *(Beat.)* Oh, he's got a frying pan out. Maybe we *will* be here for a while.

BO: He'll fire me if he knows I broke into his house!

LUKE: Well. We'll just wait it out.

BO: Stupid money. I should have just waited till Monday to get it.

LUKE: We didn't have any plans tonight anyway, so . . .

BO: That's easy for you to say.

LUKE: What? *Did* you have plans tonight?

BO: Sort of. Yeah.

LUKE: With who? I thought you had to study for that test.

BO: Nothing, Luke. It was just this little thing. With some people.

LUKE: Who?

BO: Just some people. You wouldn't like them. Trust me.

> *(LUKE just shrugs and looks through the peephole.)*

STRAVINSKY: Where the hell is my spatula? That boy is worthless.

LUKE: I can't believe you did this. How can he *not* know this is here?

BO: Are you kidding me? Stravinsky's clueless. He never comes in here. I told you, I do all the cooking.

  (Pause.)

LUKE: What's he like?

BO: He's a pain in the American ass. He's grumpy. Irritable. Always wants his food served in his study, on a stupid little tray. *Has* to have his horseradish and cloves.

LUKE: Seriously?

BO: Seriously. To be honest, we haven't been getting along. He's always mad at something. He plays that loud classical music while I'm cooking, and it just gets on my last nerve. Always tells me I don't return things to *where they belong.* He's annoying.

LUKE: Well, maybe he *is* a pain. But be thankful you've got a job, Bo.

  (STRAVINSKY discovers the spilled pencils.)

STRAVINSKY: What the hell . . . ? That boy . . . .

BO: Whatever.

LUKE: *(Looking through the peephole.)* I'm serious. Richard Nixon's done nothing for my job status. I'd love to work somewhere like this. I'd serve up that horseradish with a golden spoon!

STRAVINSKY: *(Picking up the pencils.)* I cannot believe this. That *idiot.*

LUKE: Um. I think he's discovered our little mess.

BO: Damn! Did he?

LUKE: Yeah. But he doesn't know that *you* did it.

STRAVINSKY: I'm going to kill that little bastard. Only Bo would do this and then leave it.

LUKE: Well, then again, he actually *might* know . . .

BO: *(Pacing, angry.)* I can't believe it! Luke, you're going to get me fired! This is all your fault.

LUKE: What??

BO: It is!

LUKE: How??

BO: You just *had* to come along. *Had* to see Stravinsky's house.

LUKE: Bo, you were scared to come in this house alone!

BO: Oh, I was just saying that.

LUKE: Oh, come on!

BO: It's true . . .

LUKE: *(Waving his hand.)* Ehhhh.

> *(Beat. As BO paces, LUKE suddenly notices a hanging chef's hat and puts it on. Then he quickly grabs a bottle of olive oil/condiment from the shelf, and begins to mime somebody.)*

LUKE: Hey Bo, look. Who am I?

BO: What are you doing? I don't know. Who are you?

LUKE: I'm Charlie! Come on, you know! The olive oil?? From that cooking class?

BO: Not in the mood, man. *(Looks through the peephole.)*

LUKE: Sorry. Only trying to cheer you up.

BO: It didn't work.

LUKE: Look, we'll be fine. He'll leave soon, and we'll sneak out.

STRAVINSKY: Where is my wheat bread??

BO: Aghhhh! The wheat bread!

LUKE: Huh?

BO: I was supposed to get his wheat bread yesterday and I didn't!

STRAVINSKY: That boy . . .

BO: Oh, this is terrible! I just want to get my money and get outta here!

LUKE: Well, sheesh. I could have just loaned you some money till Monday.

BO: No, it's not that. I already got paid my normal check. I . . . well, don't worry about it.

LUKE: Wait. *What?*

BO: Nothing.

LUKE: You already got paid your check?

BO: Yes.

LUKE: So what's in that envelope out there? More money?

BO: I told you, don't worry about it.

LUKE: He paid you twice? On accident?

BO: Yes. *(Pause.)* If you must know.

(Long pause. They stare at each other.)

LUKE: Wow.

BO: He's done it before. He's old. He forgets.

LUKE: Bo, that's dishonest.

BO: If he wants to pay me twice, then that's his problem!

LUKE: You should return it.

BO: And just who are you? Mother Teresa??

LUKE: Um. No. But—

BO: So mind your own business, Luke! It's my money!

LUKE: *(Quietly.)* Okay.

BO: It's his fault that he paid me twice. He's rich. He can afford it! *(Pause.)* Anyway, this is my situation, not yours.

LUKE: *(Defeated.)* I'll be quiet about it.

BO: *(Checking the peephole.)* Now, come on. We gotta figure out how to get outta here. We need a plan. *(Pause as he watches. STRAVINSKY wipes his hands, looks around for something that isn't there.)* Hang on. He may be about to leave.

LUKE: Really? *(Walking over.)*

BO: Yeah, take a look. He looks like he forgot something.

(The telephone rings.)

LUKE: The phone!

BO: Hallelujah!!

(STRAVINSKY exits.)

LUKE: Finally!

BO: He's leaving! Okay, look, here's what we'll do. I'll go out first and then ring the doorbell. Then, you sneak out the back while he's distracted.

LUKE: Why can't we both go out?

BO: Too risky! You'll make too much noise.

LUKE: Aww.

BO: I'll go first! I'll pretend that I forgot I was off today. Okay?

LUKE: Uh, yeah.

BO: Okay, I'm going!
    (Starts to exit.)
Remember, I'll go out the front and then ring the bell. When Stravinsky is talking to me, you go out!

LUKE: Out the front door, right?

BO: No, *you* go out the back door!

LUKE: Oh! Where is that?

BO: It's in the back, you dumb-ass.

LUKE: Oh, right!

    (BO exits hurriedly. Pause, then LUKE comes out,
    still wearing the chef hat, and begins to exit through
    the front door. Confused, he turns around to retreat,
    and he knocks over something. Enter
    STRAVINSKY.)

STRAVINSKY: Uh . . . yes?? Can I help you?

LUKE: Oh, hello there! So sorry—I just—you know, I just came on in. Oh, here, I knocked over something. *(Bends to pick it up.)*

STRAVINSKY: You are the new chef from the referral service?

LUKE: Oh . . . oh, *yes*! Yes, I am. I'm sorry, I didn't wait, I just decided to come on in and get started!

STRAVINSKY: Well, that's fine, I guess. I didn't expect you until tomorrow.

(The doorbell rings.)

LUKE: Oh, well, you know, I'm always early! No sir, I *hate* being late.

STRAVINSKY: *(Notices his hat.)* I see. You came dressed for work. I like that.

LUKE: Oh, this old thing? Oh, well, you know, dress for success!

STRAVINSKY: I see. Tell me about yourself.

LUKE: Well, I'm a college student. And I'm also a chef. And like I said, I'm always on time.

STRAVINSKY: So you've said.

(Doorbell rings again.)

LUKE: Uh, aren't you going to get that?

STRAVINSKY: No. It's probably just my idiot neighbor. He's always wanting to borrow a cup of sugar or something.

LUKE: Oh. Okay.

STRAVINSKY: Tell me, do you mind loud music in the house while you work?

LUKE: Oh, are you kidding me? I just love music of all kinds. Especially classical music! The timpani and those trombones!

STRAVINSKY: Splendid. Splendid. What about making a mess? Do you make a mess when you work?

LUKE: I'm the cleanest chef you'll lay eyes on. And you know what else I do?

STRAVINSKY: What?

LUKE: I return things to where they *belong*. Everything has a place, right?

STRAVINSKY: Everything. And never forget that!!

LUKE: Never! *(Salutes him Russian-style.)*

STRAVINSKY: You know Russian salute?

LUKE: Oh, my father studied Russian military history. I know all about it.

STRAVINSKY: Well. Good. There is one thing. But first: what is your name?

LUKE: Luke.

STRAVINSKY: There is one thing I've learned, Mr. Luke.

LUKE: What is that?

STRAVINSKY: Loyalty is hard to find.

LUKE: I know. I agree.

STRAVINSKY: A good loyal worker, or a good loyal friend. They are hard to find.

LUKE: I COMPLETELY agree.

STRAVINSKY: So we'll see how you do. I didn't expect you until tomorrow, but I suppose we can get started. I was just getting dinner started. Do you know botvinya?

LUKE: Botvinya? It's my favorite!

STRAVINSKY: Well, it's my least favorite.

LUKE: Oh.

(The doorbell rings again.)

STRAVINSKY: But tonight I wanted it for some reason. Perhaps you can finish it up. *(Pointing to the food/frying pan.)* Isn't life strange? We don't eat certain things for a long time. And then out of nowhere we have the urge to eat them again. *(He laughs.)* Who know what surprises each day will bring?

LUKE: You can say that again!

(Once again, the doorbell rings.)

STRAVINSKY: Okay, hop to it!

LUKE: Yes sir! Oh, uh, aren't you going to get the door?

STRAVINSKY: No. I told you, it's probably just my neighbor. *(He says a well-known expression in Russian here.)*

LUKE: Uh . . . what does that mean?

STRAVINSKY: Old Russian expression. In English it simply means 'no jackasses are welcome here.'

LUKE: Okay!

STRAVINSKY: Mr. Luke . . . *(He presses the play button on the radio/boombox. A piece of classical music begins to play.)* I've got a good feeling about you.

(Exits. Luke, still surprised, begins to prepare the meal. He waves his hands merrily, in time to the music. ** BO may look through a window, in shock, if this is possible *** End of play.)

HONORING THE HIJACKER

- -

A ten-minute play for college students

by
John Glass

☞ ☞

www.studentplays.org
john@studentplays.org

Honoring the Hijacker

☆ **Characters** ☆

JOEL	Twenties/thirties. Jolly but aggressive.
JOHN	Twenties/thirties.
LANA	Thirties. Girlfriend/wife of Billy.
BILLY	Thirties.
AIRLINE EMPLOYEE	Any gender. Any age. Tiny role at end.

The time is the winter of 1981, the setting is a large front room of a cabin in the rural outskirts of Portland, Oregon. It is the ten-year celebration of D.B. Cooper, and there is a large banner hanging in the background that reads *Long Live D.B. Cooper*! There are a few candles and lanterns throughout the room, and there are many opened bottles of alcohol/beer.

It is after midnight and everyone is seated around a table, slowly sipping alcohol. LANA and BILLY are a couple, and should sit together. They have been here all night, and the rest of the participants have all turned in. There are several candles/kerosene lamps on the table. The characters are dressed in winter clothing. Everyone is generally tipsy/drowsy.

(Before the lights go up, the following is to be read from the typical voice of a morning radio newscaster from 1981. There may be busy typewriter hubbub in the background, or other classic newsroom noises to enhance the mood as this is read.)

"Ten years ago the passengers of Northwest Orient Airlines flight 305 had the experience of their lives when one of its passengers hijacked the plane. The plane was hijacked in the airspace between Portland, Oregon, and Seattle, Washington, and was forced to land at Seattle-Tacoma Airport, where the hijacker collected 200,000 dollars in ransom money. He also demanded several parachutes. He then ordered the plane airborne again, this time with the destination of Mexico City. But within a half-hour of takeoff, the hijacker, using one of the parachutes, jumped from the plane. Although he was thought to have landed somewhere south of Mount St. Helens, the hijacker was never found. The man's name was D. B. Cooper, and has since achieved a kind of cult status for rebels and anti-establishment everywhere. Festivals are held around the country every year to commemorate the legend of D.B. Cooper, and 1981 is proving to be no different. *(Pause.)* In other news, Portland is seeing its share of cold weather and . . . *(voice fades)*."

At RISE: Everyone is seated around a large table, and they are all drowsy and tipsy. It is late, after midnight.

JOEL: It was *David* Cooper! Not D.B. Cooper!

JOHN: Are you sure?

JOEL: Yes, I'm sure!

LANA: David, yeah. I heard you guys arguing about that.

JOEL: I learned about it in a psychology class. The press had it all wrong. His real name was David, not D.B. They screwed it up when the story first broke.

JOHN: Wow.

JOEL: And you're right, we really got into it over that. Me and those jackasses from Seattle.

BILLY: Tell me about it. You were up in arms.

JOHN: Those guys were from Seattle? The ones that sat in the corner, drinking Wild Turkey?

JOEL: Yes.

LANA: *(To JOEL.)* They kept saying you looked like D.B.

JOEL: Idiots. They didn't know a thing about D.B. Cooper. *David* Cooper. They told me he had children, which was a lie. D.B. never had kids.

BILLY: You sure seem like the expert.

JOEL: Well, I told you, I studied him in class.
(Beat. He bristles.)
This festival thing is only one weekend of the year and those morons couldn't even last past midnight. On the ten-year anniversary! Only a real trooper would stay up in honor of what Mr. Cooper did.
(Checks his watch).
As a matter of fact, ten years ago this very hour. Ten years ago our man was parachuting down, somewhere over the Pacific Northwest, with 200,000 dollars crammed in his jumpsuit. That's why we're here, isn't it?
(Raises glass in a toast. They reluctantly join in.)
Come on, we're the only ones still awake. Here's to our hijacker!!

JOHN: Hear hear!

JOEL: Someone who actually beat the system!

(BILLY yawns.)

JOEL: You aren't tired, are you?

BILLY: Uh, no. No!

JOEL: Hmmpph. *(Beat. To LANA.)* So . . . I want to hear more about this. Your cousin's neighbor was actually on the same flight with D.B.?

LANA: Yep. She's kind of how I got into it all this.

BILLY: *(Pointing to LANA.)* I didn't even know about D.B. Cooper until I met her.

LANA: Now he's the biggest fan I know.

JOHN: *(To LANA.)* Did you ever talk to her about it? Did she live here, in Portland?

LANA: My cousin's neighbor? Yeah, she's local. *(Points to BILLY.)* Same as us two. She sold her house and moved away years ago but we talked about it a few times. She said she didn't talk to D.B. on the flight but she sat very close to him. He was just a guy. Very normal. *(She pauses, in thought.)* D.B. was just tired of authority in general. You know, rules, regulations. I don't blame him a bit for what he did. I never liked people that were always telling me what to do.

JOHN: What do you mean?

LANA: Oh, you know. Teachers from my high school. My church, when I was a kid. Everything. My first husband. Shit, just about every boss I've ever had.

JOHN: D.B. reminds you of yourself, huh?

LANA: What? Uh, well, yes. Yes, he does, in that regard.

JOHN: You kind of consider yourself the rebellious sort?

LANA: Yeah. *(Pause.)* Why?

JOHN: Oh, I don't know. Seems like you've been that way all night. Seems like everybody else here has too.

LANA: Anything wrong with that?

JOHN: No. Of course not.

LANA: That's kind of why we're here, right? To celebrate anti-authority types . . ?

JOHN: Yep.

BILLY: *(To JOEL)* You'll have to forgive me . . . but I'm sitting here staring at you. Those guys were right. You actually do look a lot like those pictures of D.B.!

JOEL: So I'm told.

JOHN: You think he does? He's kind of young, compared to D.B.

BILLY: I really do.

JOEL: *(To BILLY.)* Anything the matter with that?

BILLY: No.

JOEL: Are you sure?
(Pause as he gets up and walks over to his backpack.)
So what if I look a little like D.B.?
(Reaches into backpack for something.)
Oh well . . . since you've blown my cover, I'll have to do something about it.

(BILLY quickly stands, suspecting something. JOEL yanks his hand out, holding nothing. He bursts into laughter, points at them.)

JOEL: Ha ha! I got you guys!

BILLY: Damn . . .

JOEL: I got all of you! Come on, get into the hijacking spirit!

LANA: Wow. You did get me.

JOHN: Yeah. Me too.

JOEL: Sorry about that! *(More laughter as he sits, gradually calms down.)* That was good. Oh, man. Wow. *(Beat.)* Well . . . you talk about being a true soldier of D.B. Cooper. But only a real fan would have something like this. *(Pulls out a glass from his jacket.)*

JOHN: Wow.

BILLY: What is that?

JOEL: It's D.B.'s scotch glass.

BILLY: Is that the glass he drank from? On the flight?

JOEL: Yep. One and the same.

JOHN: How the hell did you get that? *(Takes it, holds it.)*

JOEL: There was an auction in Tacoma last year of his things from the flight. His tie clip. His lighter.

BILLY: I read about that. I almost went.

JOEL: Yep. Some guy from LA came in and bought almost everything. I got this. *(Taking the glass back, sets it down. Looks at LANA.)* So, lady, you aren't the only one here that's angry at the system. This is just *one* of my ways of honoring our hijacker. The only professional thief to ever jump from an airplane and never be caught! The only unsolved case of air piracy in U.S. history!

LANA: What other ways do you have?

JOEL: What?

LANA: You just said this was only *one* of your ways of honoring him. What other ways do you have?

JOEL: Oh. Well, that's for me to know, and you to find out.

JOHN: I had the idea of going up to Vancouver and try to dig up some more of that money they uncovered last year. Did you all hear about that?

JOEL: Oh, yeah. On the banks of the Columbia River?

JOHN: Yes.

JOEL: They never proved that was his money.

BILLY: I remember that. Why didn't you do it?

JOHN: Well, I was sitting in this boring history class one morning, planning my trip. But then I suddenly remembered that I had a set of twins at home.

LANA: Twins? I thought you were a college student.

JOHN: I am. But I'm a married college student.

JOEL: A family guy, huh? Hmmph.

JOHN: Yep. So yeah, I came to my senses. Plus, it wouldn't have been fair to my wife if I had taken off like that. She has the kids all the time. So it never happened. Real bummer.

BILLY: You let your kids stand in the way of making a trip like that? That's not a good enough reason.

JOHN: Excuse me?

BILLY: *(Pointing at LANA.)* Her brother has three children and he comes to this D.B. festival every year. And he's from Utah! You can't let children get in the way of something cool like that.

JOHN: Well, that's different. I live down in Eugene, not Portland. Vancouver is a good drive from my house. It's not just a weekend excursion.

LANA: True. Good point.

JOHN: I can't just up and leave my wife with a pair of infants. She works hard, too.

BILLY: *(Dismissively.)* Ahhh.

JOEL: *(To BILLY.)* You haven't done anything like that.

JOHN: Yeah!

LANA: How do you know what he's done?

JOHN: Well . . . has he?

BILLY: Please. I've done plenty. I know one thing: I wouldn't let family get in the way of something I was interested in.

JOEL: *(To BILLY.)* Well . . . . what have you done? *(Pointing to JOHN.)* At least this guy had the idea of going and seeing about that buried money. Me, I'm holding my pride and joy right here. *(Points at the glass.)* What the hell's your story?

BILLY: What's my story?

JOEL: That's what I said.

LANA: Oh, don't get him going. He's got a lot of stories.

BILLY: You don't want to go there, pal. You just don't.

LANA: Maybe we're getting a little too serious here.

JOHN: I like how things are progressing.

JOEL: And I'd like to hear his story.

LANA: No, maybe we all need to cool off a bit.

JOHN: Hang on, we're actually getting somewhere here!

LANA: *(Slides chair back, starts to stand.)* No, I think you guys are getting way too testy and out of control.

JOHN: Well, maybe we NEED TO BE TESTY AND OUT OF CONTROL!! *(Stands and kicks his chair to the side.)* RIGHT??

(A long awkward pause.)

LANA: What the hell are you doing?

(JOHN bursts into laughter and points at them.)

JOHN: Oh, that was great! You should have seen your faces!!

LANA: Son of a bitch . . .

JOEL: Damn.

JOHN: Oh, man! *(More laughter.)*

BILLY: Maybe this *has* been enough for one night.

JOHN: I need another drink!

JOEL: You're good, friend. That was a good one. You upstaged me.

JOHN: Yeah?

JOEL: Oh yeah.

JOHN: Well, if you like that, you're definitely going to like this.

> *(Pulls a gun from inside his coat pocket and points it at them.)*

Okay. Nobody say a word. Put your wallets on the table. All of you.

> *(Pause. They are in instant shock.)*

JOEL: You can't be serious.

JOHN: Did you HEAR WHAT I SAID? Put your wallets on the TABLE. And as you do, SHUT UP!! *(He sticks the barrel right into JOEL's face.)* NOW.

> *(The men toss their wallets across the table to him.)*

JOHN: You too, toots. I saw your little coin purse thingie when you were buying drinks at the bar, earlier. Pink and white, I believe? Several hundreds neatly tucked away in it? Toss it!

> *(She does and JOHN takes it while pulling out a roll of duct tape.)*

Good girl. Now, tie your old man's hands up, toots. Tie them TIGHT.

> *(She begins to do this.)*

JOHN: You were right, Pops. D.B. never had any children. But he sure as hell had a nephew. A nephew that never had a fair break at anything. A nephew that doesn't have time to wait for a college degree. I've been waiting for this ten-year anniversary forever!

LANA: You should really re-think this.

JOHN: *(Sticking gun right in her face.)* What will it take to SHUT YOU UP??
        (Pause. She shuts up.)
That's better. And is this really how you imbeciles honor my uncle? Some lame-ass cabin party in the rural backwoods of Portland, Oregon? What a joke. D.B. would laugh at this. Honoring the hijacker, my ass. You people are in such a hurry to prove your so-called 'toughness' that it's ridiculous! LET'S HURRY IT UP WITH THE TAPE!!

JOEL: Guy, is this really worth it? A small-time robbery?

JOHN: *(Puts a piece of tape over JOEL's mouth.)* Please. You think this is my first rodeo? With what I've already done, I won't have any worries for a long time. This is just the icing on the cake. *(Admiring the tape.)* There. Nice and tight. Much better. Yep, there's only one true way to honor my uncle on this anniversary. I'm here to finish what he started. HURRY WITH THE TAPE!
        (Takes the glass from the table.)
I'll relieve you of this. Okay, let's go, folks. I have a nice, big closet to stick you all in. Move!

        *(He quickly ushers them offstage with the gun.
        Lights fade to black. Long pause. The stage remains*

dark, and then we hear the sounds of a typical
airport, people milling about, airplane traffic, etc.
The following voice is spoken in total darkness.)

INTERCOM VOICE: Flight 2035, Seattle to Buenos Aires, now boarding. Flight 2035, Seattle to Buenos Aires, now boarding.

(One light goes up on an airline employee. He is
standing behind a small table that
resembles a counter at an airport, looking over
paperwork/tickets, etc. After a moment JOHN
enters, wearing a dress jacket and sunglasses,
carrying a small suitcase. He is also carrying the
scotch glass, with an iced beverage inside.)

JOHN: Good morning. Hope I still made it!

TICKET PERSONNEL: Good morning! Oh yes, there's time. You made it.

JOHN: Good. *(Passing him his ticket.)* Here you go . . .

TICKET PERSONNEL: Thank you. Let's see . . . *(Looks over ticket, stamps it with stamper.)* Okay. Here you go. Seat 14A. You are all set Mr. Cooper.

JOHN: Great, thank you very much. *(Beat.)* Um, is it okay if I carry my drink on the flight?

TICKET PERSONNEL: I think so, yeah. That shouldn't be a problem at all.

JOHN: Thank you. This glass . . . was a gift, and it's kind of personal to me.

TICKET PERSONNEL: Well then, you should definitely hang on to it!

JOHN: Thank you.

TICKET PERSONNEL: Enjoy your flight, sir!

JOHN: I intend to!

(He exits in a hurry. The sounds of the airport go on for a moment more and then gradually fade. Lights fade. End of play.)

☞ **More from Student Plays** ☜

Othello's Just Another Fellow

Dramedy. **Grades 5-7.** 25-35 minutes. 8 actors: 4 males, 3 females, one teacher (or student portraying a teacher) 3 to 5 extras, if needed. ****A Latino-themed play****

A group of students are involved in a school production of *Othello*, but one of them is disturbed about the lack of diversity in the play. He takes certain steps to disrupt the play but in the end is encouraged by the others to try and make a difference in another, more constructive way. A lesson is learned, and the production is saved from disaster!

Pagasqueeny's Pantry

Comedy. **Middle/High School.** 15-20 minutes. 6 actors: 3 females, 2 males. One student (or a teacher) plays the comical role of the elderly Mr. Pagasqueeny.

Three friends sneak into Mr. Pagasqueeny's home to get something that one of them left behind. But in walks Pagasqueeny and they must hide in the pantry! In this comical play, a lesson is learned about honesty and trust, but it takes a heated discussion in the pantry and a subsequent attempt to escape to find this out!

Una Carta de Abuelo

Dramedy. **Middle/High School.** 35-45 minutes. 10 actors: 1 teacher, 5 females, 4 males. (With the option of 4-5 extra actors in two scenes.) ****A Latino-themed play****

Two cousins discover an old letter in their late grandfather's comic collection that they think leads to treasure! The cousins often butt heads, with one believing that he is more "Mexican," the other believing that some people make too much of a fuss about "being Mexican." Thus, they form their *own* groups in search of what Grandpa hid long ago. But what they find is actually worth more than merely silver or gold.

Barbecue at the Prom!

Dramedy. **Grades 5-8.** 25-35 minutes. 6 actors: 3 females, 3 males

It's a classic tale of guys versus girls! It's a prom committee, and everybody is supposed to work together but differences and opinions get in the way, causing the guys and girls to form their groups. For the end-of-the-year prom, one side wants pasta and lace, the other wants sports and barbecue! The two groups square off but eventually work together, demonstrating the importance of cooperation and compromise.

Going to Guatemala

Dramedy. **High School.** 50-60 minutes. 11 actors. 6 males, 5 females.   ****A Latino-themed play****

A Latino student is chosen at the last minute to join a humanitarian group from his school that is headed to Guatemala. But since his Spanish is weak, he faces ridicule and criticism from certain peers. Jealousy and anger trickle throughout the campus as the trip approaches, and the social buzz of the high school becomes even more hectic when the student's trip money is stolen on campus, jeopardizing his trip.

Stravinsky's Kitchen

Comedy. **High School/College.** 12-15 minutes. 3 actors: 3 males (or females).

Two friends secretly enter the home of an employer to obtain a forgotten object but the homeowner abruptly arrives home while they are there. As they hide in the kitchen's pantry and plot their getaway, the two talk and eventually argue, exposing the true colors of one of them. Upon their hasty exit a mistake is made, and one of them capitalizes on this mistake, resulting in his/her fortune.

Forty Whacks

Drama. Spooky. **High School/College.** 25-35 minutes. 3 actors: 2 females, 1 male.

A pair of siblings have inherited the Lizzie Borden Bed and Breakfast in New England. Although the business was run for decades in a quiet, respectable fashion, one of the siblings is over-ambitious, wanting to unearth an alleged piece of buried evidence within the house. This brings about a chilly tension between brother and sister, and perhaps within the house itself.

John Calhoun and a Thief

Drama. **College.** 35-40 minutes. 3 actors: 2 females, 1 male.

Kicked out of a university PhD program, a bitter and dejected female lifts from the library archives original copies of John Calhoun's personal documents. Counseled and consoled by her roommates, her conscience slowly gets to her; but as she seeks entry to other universities her luck turns to worse, and the subsequent decisions she makes regarding the historic papers cause this one-act play to become darker, if not funnier.

Honoring the Hijacker

Drama. **College.** 12-15 minutes. 4 actors: 2 females, 2 males.

It's 1981, the ten-year anniversary of the famed hijacker D.B. Cooper. The play's four characters are attending a "D.B. Festival" and have stayed up very late, outlasting everybody else. The late night chit-chat goes from pranks and jokes to outright volatility, and suddenly this get-together becomes something that three of the four characters didn't bargain for.

It's a Super Day at Sammy's!

Comedy. **Middle or High School.** 35-40 minutes. 9 actors: 5 females, 4 males (4 possible adults).

Jodi has found a summer job at a travel agency. But her three younger siblings can't seem to live without her! They call her at the office incessantly, which interferes with the work. The standard telephone greeting "It's a super day at Sammy's!" becomes a repeated theme of this comedy, as Jodi struggles to reach a balance between her job and her nagging siblings

Three Tenners

Comedy/Drama. **Elementary through High School.** Three Ten-Minute Plays.

Three Creepy Plays

Drama. **Middle School through College.** Three short 'creepy' plays.

Hockey Masks in Hueytown

Drama. Spooky. **High School/College.** 20-25 minutes. 4 actors: 2 males, 2 females.

Driving home for Thanksgiving break, four college students stop off in a small rural town to retrieve one of the student's old family pictures. They reluctantly enter the empty home of his deceased uncle, a former producer for the Friday the 13th movies. Strange objects are found during their search . . but when a hockey mask surfaces, everything really goes sideways.

The Witch Makes Five

Drama. Spooky. **High School.** 10 minutes. 4 actors: 2 males, 2 females.

After a bizarre group camping trip, a student is checked into a youth mental facility . When she is visited by the other members of the trip, memories of the weekend trickle out . . . and horrific things begin to happen.

Mrs. Calapooza and the Culebra

Dramedy. **Grades 5-8.** 10 minutes. 5 actors: 3 females, 2 males.

Fed up with their grouchy teacher's classroom ways, four students complain and bicker back and forth during a Spanish quiz. The situation grows worse when the friends discover that one of them has pulled the ultimate prank on the teacher.

Raiders of the Lost Rakasa

Dramedy. **Grades 5-8.** 10 minutes. 7 actors: 4 females, 3 males.

Seven young explorers arrive at a cave in a far-off land in search of the great "Rakasa." They find what they want . . . along with a few of the cave's unexpected surprises.